Big and Small

by Rod Theodorou and Carole Telford

Contents

Heinemann

First published in Great Britain by Heinemann Library
an imprint of Heinemann Publishers (Oxford) Ltd
Halley Court, Jordan Hill, Oxford OX2 8EJ

MADRID ATHENS PARIS FLORENCE PRAGUE WARSAW
PORTSMOUTH NH CHICAGO SAO PAULO SINGAPORE TOKYO
MELBOURNE AUCKLAND IBADAN GABORONE JOHANNESBURG

Illustrations by Gwen Tourret and Trevor Dunton
Colour reproduction by Track QSP
Printed in China

99 98 97 96
10 9 8 7 6 5 4 3 2 1

ISBN 0 431 06393 1

British Library Cataloguing in Publication Data
Telford, Carole
 Big and Small. – (Animal Opposites Series)
 I. Title II. Theodorou, Rod III. Series
 591

Photographic acknowledgements
Babs and Bert Wells/OSF p5 *left*, back cover; Manis Wildlife Films/OSF p5 *right*; Hans Reinhard/Bruce Coleman p6
left; Martyn Colbeck/OSF pp6 *right*, 8, 14, 18 *bottom*, 20; Brian Rogers/Biofotos p7 *left*; Colin Milkins/OSF p7 *right*;
C W Helliwell/OSF p9 *top left*; John Cooke/OSF p9 *bottom left*; J A L Cooke/OSF pp9 *right*, 15, 17, 19 *left*, 21;
Ajay Desai/OSF p10; Neil Bromhall/OSF p11; Jeanne Drake/Tony Stone Images p12; K G Vock/Okapia/OSF p13;
Rafi Ben-Shahar/OSF p16; Johan Elzenga/Tony Stone Worldwide p18 *top*; James H Robinson/OSF p19 *right*
Front cover: Dianne Blell Photography *left*; Michael Fogden/OSF *right*

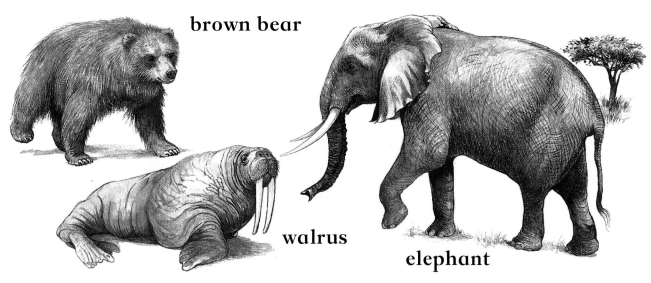

brown bear

walrus

elephant

Some animals are big.
Some animals are small.

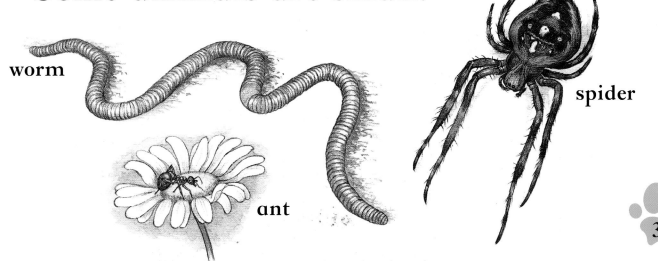

worm

ant

spider

3

These are
elephants.
Elephants
are very big
and slow.

This is an ant.
Ants are very small
and move quickly.

eye

jaw

5

There are
two kinds of
elephants.

Asian elephant

African elephant

They are
Asian elephants
and African
elephants.

6

There are lots of different
kinds of ants.
Ants live all over the world.

leaf-cutter ant

black ant

7

Elephants live together in herds.
The oldest cow elephant leads
the herd.

calf   cow

wood ant nest

Thousands of ants
live together in a nest.
Every nest has a
few big queen ants.

army
ant
queen

worker   soldier

Elephants are very strong.
An elephant can lift up a heavy log.

Ants are strong, too.
This ant can carry a big
piece of plant.

Elephants eat lots of plants and drink lots of water.
An elephant drinks 25 buckets of water a day!

Some ants eat plants.
Most ants eat other creatures.

An elephant
can pull down
branches from
trees to eat
the leaves.

Ants work together to carry
leaves back to their nest.

Elephants stick out their ears to
make their heads look bigger.
This frightens away their enemies.

Soldier ants fight off enemies.
They can bite or squirt acid.

Elephant mothers have one baby every three years.

Mothers feed their babies with milk for four years.

Every year, a queen ant lays
thousands of eggs.
Worker ants look after the eggs.

queen leaf-cutter ant

Baby elephants love to play.

Ants never play.
They are always hard at work.

AMAZING FACTS!

An elephant's toe-nail is bigger than a child's hand.

Sometimes elephants make sunhats out of leafy branches.

There may be up
to half a million
ants in one nest!

Leaf-cutter ants
can strip a tree
bare in one night!

Index